RIYADH

text by ANTHONY GUISE
photographed by CHRIS GENT

RIYADH

STACEY INTERNATIONAL
LONDON AND NEW JERSEY

Editor Nicholas Drake

Design Keith Savage

Riyadh
Stacey International
128 Kensington Church Street, London W8 4BH
Telex: 298768 STACEY G

171 First Avenue, Atlantic Highlands
New Jersey 07716, USA
Telex: 752233 HILARIOUS

British Library Cataloguing in Publication Data

Gent, Chris
Riyadh.
1. Riyadh (Saudi Arabia) – Description – Views
I. Title   II. Guise, Anthony
953'.8   DS248.R5

ISBN 0-905743-53-9

Library of Congress Cataloguing in Publication Information

Guise, Anthony, 1940-
Riyadh

1. Riyadh (Saudi Arabia) – Description – Views.
I. Title
DS248.R5G85   1987   953'.8   87-7084

Set in Linotronic Baskerville by
SX Composing Limited, Essex, England.
Colour originations by
Regent Publishing Services Ltd..
Printed and bound by
Leefung-Asco Printers Ltd.

The Publishers are grateful to the following organisations and
individuals for their assistance and advice in the preparation
of this book:

H.E. Abdullah Al-Ali Al-Nuaim, Mayor of Riyadh; The
Ministry of Information, Riyadh; the Arab-British Chamber
of Commerce; S.M. Tassan, Director General, KKIA; Husni
Samman, Supervisor, and Michael Foley, KKIA Media
Production Services. Special thanks to Muhammad Al
Shabeeb.

The Publishers also wish to acknowledge the following
publications which have been useful in the preparation of this
book:

Riyadh, The City of the Future King Saud University Press 1986;
H.St John Philby The Heart of Arabia London 1922; W.G.
Palgrave Narrative of a Year's Journey Through Central and Eastern
Arabia London 1868.

Vesti Corporation of Boston provided the design, fabrication
and delivery of the stained glass, carved doors, carved stone,
ceramic mosaic, and frieze, seen below and opposite, and on
pages 52 and 72-5 (Wayne Andersen, President; Leslie
Chabot, Vice President and Project Manager; Edman
Avasian and Brian Clarke, principal designers).

Principal Photographer: Chris Gent
All photographs by Chris Gent except:
Vesti Corporation 4, 5, 72(2), 73(2), 74(7), 75(3); Topham
Picture Library 9; H.E. Abdullah Al-Ali Al-Nuaim 11, 13, 14,
18(2); H M Shalabi (IPA) 16; Richard Bryant/ARCAID 16,
28(2) 29(2); François Geunet/GAMMA (Frank Spooner
Pictures) 34, 35, 80, 81(2), 82; KKIA Media
Production Services 52(2), 53(2), 68, 69(2), 70, 71(2), 76-77,
78; Islamic Press Agency 20, 61; PIC Photos Ltd 60;
Tom Gable/ABCL 72; The Hutchison Library 20, 79, 83, 84;
Bernard Gerard (The Hutchison Library) 82; TRIP/IPA
87(2), 102, 105; Helene Rogers/TRIP 102(2), 103; M S Al
Shabeeb 56, 100 (2), 101(3), 102(2), 103, 110, 111(2); Oger
85(2), 89(2); Aljomaih & Shell Lubricating Oil Co Ltd
103(2), 105(2).

Half title: *Central Riyadh's landmark – in the Murabba area – is the
water tower. Riyadh is supplied by its wadis, dams, wells, geological
aquifers, desalinated water piped from Jubail, and purified waste
water.*

Title page: *At the Youth Welfare Stadium in Malaz fans gather to
cheer on the Riyadh football team.*

This page and opposite: *At the mosque at King Khalid Airport, the
dome – 33 metres across – "floats" above the rest of the building on a
frame of clear glass. The mahogany doors with their intricate Islamic
carvings were made in Jeddah.*

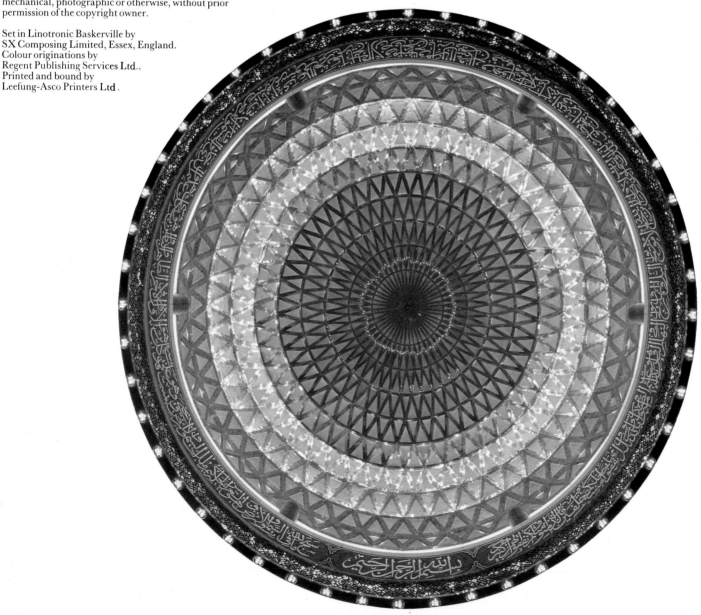

CONTENTS

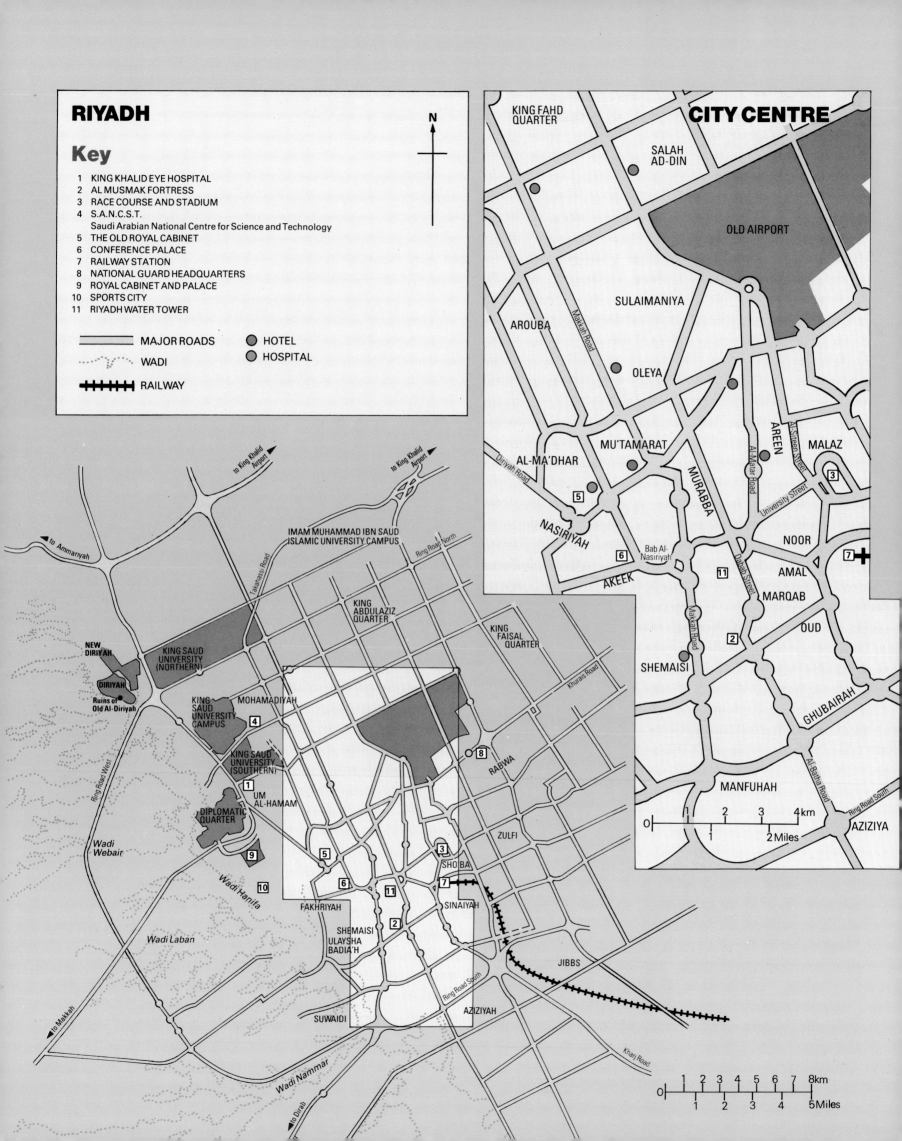

RIYADH

Key

1 KING KHALID EYE HOSPITAL
2 AL MUSMAK FORTRESS
3 RACE COURSE AND STADIUM
4 S.A.N.C.S.T.
  Saudi Arabian National Centre for Science and Technology
5 THE OLD ROYAL CABINET
6 CONFERENCE PALACE
7 RAILWAY STATION
8 NATIONAL GUARD HEADQUARTERS
9 ROYAL CABINET AND PALACE
10 SPORTS CITY
11 RIYADH WATER TOWER

	MAJOR ROADS	⬤ HOTEL
....	WADI	⬤ HOSPITAL
┼┼┼┼┼	RAILWAY	

N

CITY CENTRE

KING FAHD QUARTER

SALAH AD-DIN

OLD AIRPORT

SULAIMANIYA

AROUBA

OLEYA

Makkah Road

Diriyah Road

MU'TAMARAT

AREEN

MALAZ

Al-Steen Street

MURABBA

AL-MA'DHAR

Al-Matar Road

University Street

⑤

NASIRIYAH

Bab Al-Nasiriyah

⑥

NOOR

AKEEK

⑪

Dabab Street

AMAL

⑦

MARQAB

⑫

OUD

Makkah Road

SHEMAISI

GHUBAIRAH

MANFUHAH

Al-Batha Road

Ring Road South

AZIZIYA

0 1 2 3 4km
0   1   2 Miles

to King Khalid Airport

to King Khalid Airport

to Ammariyah

IMAM MUHAMMAD IBN SAUD ISLAMIC UNIVERSITY CAMPUS

Takhassi Road

Ring Road North

KING ABDULAZIZ QUARTER

NEW DIRIYAH

KING SAUD UNIVERSITY (NORTHERN)

DIRIYAH

Ruins of Old Al-Diriyah

KING SAUD UNIVERSITY CAMPUS

MOHAMADIYAH

KING FAISAL QUARTER

④

KING SAUD UNIVERSITY (SOUTHERN)

①

UM AL-HAMAM

Ring Road West

Wadi Webair

DIPLOMATIC QUARTER

⑧

Rabwa

Khurais Road

ZULFI

⑨

Wadi Hanifa

⑩

⑤

⑥

③

SHOBA

⑪

⑦

FAKHRIYAH

SINAIYAH

②

Wadi Laban

SHEMAISI ULAYSHA BADIA'H

JIBBS

to Makkah

Ring Road South

SUWAIDI

AZIZIYAH

Wadi Nammar

Kharj Road

to Dirab

0 1 2 3 4 5 6 7 8km
0   1   2   3   4 5 Miles

RIYADH IN HISTORY

AN INTRODUCTION TO SAUDI ARABIA'S CAPITAL CITY

RIYADH – "Gardens"– is a twentieth-century oasis in the desert: a vision made real. Seen from the glass-encased pinnacle of the Television Tower – which is also a prominent landmark – the city lies revealed as a triumph of sophisticated town planning and construction, covering some two thousand square kilometres and supporting a population of one and a half million.

Modern adaptations of Najdi and Islamic motifs and styles prevail amid the architectural panoply of the new official buildings and mosques and palaces and hotels, office buildings, apartment blocks, the water towers and factories. These elegant structures of glass and steel and concrete, interspersed with minarets, rise out of a pattern of residential, commercial and industrial precincts with their tree-lined boulevards, sweeping flyovers, and plazas and green parks shuttered against the sun by the foliage of trees.

Riyadh is also a city of history, reaching back many hundreds of years – yet a history which abuts our own times. For as recently as half a century ago, some while after King Abdul Aziz al Saud proclaimed the founding of his Kingdom

The National Guard, headquartered in Riyadh, an integral part of today's defence structure, descends directly from the military force built up

with Riyadh as its capital, the city was not much more than seven hundred metres from end to end, and still a dense labyrinth of narrow streets and earth-brick buildings, and most of it still contained within a thick, seven-metre defensive wall, skirted by date palms and small clusters of villages. Beyond that, the desert.

It had changed little from the city described by the English traveller William Palgrave in 1863 CE. Perhaps Palgrave viewed Riyadh from Abu

by King Abdul Aziz in the first decades of the century, when all movement was on horses and camels.

Riyadh was found to be one of the few naturally fertile areas in the Kingdom outside the south-west. From this it derived its name – ar-Riyath, or "The Gardens" or "Orchards".

Mahrouq (a term which refers to the "burnt" colour of the stone), a hillock with a hole in it recently dubbed the "Camel's Eye", between Shara Matar and Shara Siteen of today's city. In those days it was some distance outside the walls: the point from which the traveller would first view the city as he approached from the north, and often the site of the last encampment before entering the city. Palgrave recorded:

"Before us stretched a wild open valley, and in its foreground, immediately below the pebbly slope on whose summit we stood, lay the capital, large and square, crowned by high towers and strong walls of defense, a mass of roofs and terraces, where overtopping all frowned the huge but irregular pile of Feysul's royal castle, and hard by it rose the scarce less conspicuous palace, built and inhabited by his eldest son, Abdullah. Other edifices too of remarkable appearance broke here and there through the maze of grey roof-tops . . . . All around for full three miles over the surrounding plain, but more especially to the west and south, waved a sea of palm-trees above green fields and well-watered gardens;

while the singing droning sound of water-wheels reached us even where we had halted, at a quarter of a mile from the nearest town walls. At the opposite side southwards, the valley opened out into the great and even more fertile plains of Yamamah, thickly dotted with groves and villages, among which the large town of Manfoohah, hardly inferior in size to Riad itself, might be clearly distinguished . . . A light moving mist, the first we had witnessed for many days, hung over the town, and bespoke the copious measure of its gardens."

"Feysul" was Faisal bin Turki, the tenth Emir, whose sons, by their rivalry, were to lose Riyadh. "Manfoohah" – Manfuhah – is an integral part of today's Riyadh.

The desert surrounding Riyadh was once the sea floor, and it is still possible to find marine fossils among the rocks and loess of the Tuwayq escarpment, on whose plateau Riyadh stands at 600 metres above sea level. Following the lifting of the tectonic plate that formed the escarpment, rivers wound their way east-

wards through a verdant landscape to the basin of today's Gulf, which drained into a sea that would become the Indian Ocean.

Petraglyphs etched on the rock faces provide vivid evidence of the antiquity of human settlement in the area. Pictures of wild boar and wild oxen as well as ibex and gazelles indicate that, in the millennia following the last Ice Age, Riyadh's Najdi plateau of Yamamah ("dove") was a region of relative verdure, and that great climatic changes have occurred in central Arabia over the past few thousand years. Even today, the nearest sand desert, the red Dahna strip, lies a good one hundred kilometres from Riyadh itself. The fine dusty loess all around can be made to bring forth, given water and the removal of excess salts.

Riyadh itself was first settled in ancient pre-Islamic days because of the chance of an oasis of fertile land offered by the confluence of two wadis, Hanifa and Batha. This meeting of seasonal

Every year, Riyadh revives the country's desert past at the Janadriyah festival, where Bedouin bring their camels loaded and caparisoned in traditional style.
Opposite: *The traveller approaching Riyadh from the west is confronted by the Tuwaiq escarpment and its remarkable outcrops.*

Once established as a desert city, Riyadh became an object of dispute. The first Saudi state under Muhammad ibn Saud (died 1765) was based at the city of Diriyah, some sixty kilometres along the Wadi Hanifa from Riyadh.

watercourses created a natural reservoir of underground water; and so despite a very dry climate and low rainfall the wells stayed replenished. Riyadh was found to be one of the few naturally fertile areas in the Kingdom outside the south-west. From this it derived its name - ar-Riyath, or "The Gardens" or "Orchards" – and became an important point along the routes traversing the peninsula east to west and vice-versa, and northward from Quryat al-Fawr.

When the name Riyadh was first used by Ibn Bishr in 1636 it referred to the ancient city of Hajar ("Defended"), the centre of the Yamamah district, which flourished during the Bani Hanifa pre-Islamic period. Some four hundred years after the coming of Islam, the name had been given to the old quarters of Hajar and the fertile lands surrounding it. Much later, in the mid-eighteenth century CE these dispersed areas were unified by a great wall, the remains of which can still be seen in parts of the city today. The palace which later became the headquarters of the emirate was built in 1704 by Dahham ibn Dawwas, and remained the seat of government for a century and a half.

Once established as a desert city, Riyadh became an object of dispute. The first Saudi state under Muhammad ibn Saud (*died* 1765) was based at the city of Diriyah, some sixty kilometres along the Wadi Hanifa from Riyadh. Powered by the new religious reform inspired by the teacher ibn Abd al-Wahhab, requiring strict adherence to the pure Faith, the emirate expanded rapidly until, by the end of the eighteenth century, it had extended its authority over the Najd. It won control of Riyadh in 1773. By the turn of the century – in 1803 – a Wahhabi army brought Makkah itself under Saudi control.

For two generations Riyadh was to enjoy peace and security, as well as firm religious discipline, as a lesser city under Saudi rule whose seat of power was still Diriyah. But the fall of Makkah affronted the Ottoman sultan, who regarded himself as guardian of the Holy Cities. Alarmed at the growth of Saudi power, he ordered his Albanian-born viceroy in Egypt, Muhammad Ali, to send armies into Arabia to recapture the Holy Cities

DIRIYAH
desert capital of the first Saudi state

The remains of the desert city of Diriyah lie on the north-western edge of modern Riyadh, near King Saud University campus built in 1984. During the eighteenth century Diriyah itself was the capital of the first Saudi state. Shortly before 1720 CE, Saud ibn Muhammad, the eponymous founder of the family, became ruler of Diriyah. Under his son Muhammad, who succeeded his father in 1725, the Saudi emirate began seven decades of extraordinary expansion. This had a powerful ideological base in the religious reform deriving from the teaching of Muhammad ibn al-Wahhab (*died* 1792), who settled in Diriyah in 1745.

This return to the purity of Islam brought good order and good government and appealed alike to the tribes and to the settled population, who together provided support for the dynasty.

By the end of the eighteenth century, Diriyah was the capital of an emirate whose Wahhabi armies had extended its authority over the Najd, gained control of Riyadh and, at its point of greatest expansion, the Holy Cities of Makkah and Medina in 1803 and 1804 respectively.

But following these conquests, and the occupation of the Hijaz region, Saudi power was seen as a threat by the Ottoman Sultan, who regarded himself as guardian of the Holy Places of the entire Muslim world. An Egyptian army under the Albanian commander Muhammad Ali was raised to defeat the Wahhabis. Consequently, Makkah and Medina were recaptured, the Najd was invaded, and finally, in 1818 CE, Diriyah itself was taken and systematically ruined.

The remains of the city, key parts of which have now been restored, are characteristic mud-brick Najdi constructions. The large palace (*top left*) dominated the city, seen from its vantage (*bottom right*). Towering wall structures and fortified walls (*bottom left*) sometimes reached a height of forty feet (*top right*).

of Makkah and Medina, and destroy the Wahhabi Saudis and their extensive state. In 1812, Egyptian forces led by Muhammad Ali's son, Tusan, took Medina and, in the following year, Makkah. Then came the long, gruelling march across Central Arabia. After a long campaign, Diriyah finally fell in 1818 and was systematically ruined.

This was the end of the first Saudi state, but not of Saudi determination; for in 1824, Turki bin Abdullah al Saud, the sixth Emir, recaptured Riyadh from Muhammad Ali's forces and established it as capital of the Najd. Turki rebuilt Riyadh's walls. He erected a Qasr – a fortified palace – in the heart of the town as a seat of government, and built a great mosque.

This was the city (then ruled by Turki's son) visited by Palgrave, who also describes the "spacious and lofty" palace of the Emir, three storeys high, and "between fifty and sixty feet from the ground to the roof parapet." There were extensive private quarters, the harem, the reception hall with its vestibule where visitors would shed their shoes and swords, a prison for state offenders, a dining room for forty guest, an "oratory" – prayer-house – for occupants of the palace, a courtyard, an arsenal and powder magazine, quarters for the "prime minister of the empire", the treasurer, the Imam, the chamberlain, and the "head artilleryman of the army".

The city was entered from north, south, east and west through immense gates, one of which, the main Thumairi Gate, has today been restored. The only open space among the maze of twisting alleys was the central market. Nearby a tiny market place was reserved for women.

The religious authorities were stern. Smoking, singing and music were banned, as were other forms of in-

Until the 1920s, Riyadh was contained within its ancient walls, surmounted by turrets, and was entered only by its six gates. (This picture, like those on pages 13 and 14, has been processed from early photographs.)

"Abdul Aziz brought in his reserve party, and then regrouped his small force in a house on the central market place, opposite the gate of the fortress. At dawn the postern gate would be opened, and maybe they could surprise the guard ..."

The Musmak palace-fort in Deira (left) *was the site of Abdul Aziz's famous coup of January 1902, when the postern gate in the great door* (above) *was rushed at dawn. Riyadh was then no more than 700 metres across* (below). *Opposite, the great mosque of Riyadh in the 1920s was a spacious rectangular enclosure divided into three cloisters, two of which were covered by low, flat roofs.*

dulgence, including the wearing of silk and jewellery, and strolling in the streets. All lights had to be extinguished after evening prayer.

Following the assassination of Turki in 1834 during a dispute between members of the Saudi family, his son Faisal managed to take power from rebels who had seized Riyadh. In the following year, Faisal appointed Abdullah ibn Ali ibn Rashid to be his governor in Ha'il; Rashid's own descendants would later on establish their own rule over the Saudi state. Between 1838 and 1843, Faisal's rule over Riyadh was again interrupted when Muhammad Ali again sent a force to invade Najd and set up another member of the Saudi family as ruler under the supervision of his agent in Riyadh. Faisal himself was taken prisoner in Cairo, but escaped and re-

established his rule with the help of Abdullah ibn Rashid.

Following Faisal's death in 1865, there was a struggle for power between two of his sons, Abdullah and Saud. This conflict allowed the Ottomans to regain control of Hasa, and Muhammad ibn Rashid, the ruler of Ha'il, to extend his power over the Saudi state by ostensibly supporting Abdullah. By the time of Abdullah's death in 1889 the Saudi state had become no more than a province of the territory ruled by the Rashidis from Ha'il. Two years later, Abdullah's son Abd ar-Rahman was expelled from Riyadh by Muhammad ibn Rashid, who appointed a puppet governor in his place. Abd ar-Rahman and his family, including his son Abdul Aziz, born in 1880, fled to Kuwait, an independent emirate.

During the 1860s the fortress of

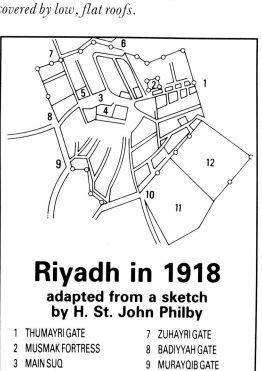

Riyadh in 1918
adapted from a sketch by H. St. John Philby

1 THUMAYRI GATE	7 ZUHAYRI GATE
2 MUSMAK FORTRESS	8 BADIYYAH GATE
3 MAIN SUQ	9 MURAYQIB GATE
4 QASR OF KING ABDUL AZIZ	10 DAKHANAH GATE
5 GREAT MOSQUE	11/12 NEW QUARTER
6 SUWAYLIM GATE	

Musmak had been built to the north-east of the Qasr. This was the fortress captured by the young Abdul Aziz early one January morning in 1902, an audacious *coup* which was to be the start of the latest restoration of the Saudi dynasty.

Today, it is the best known and most frequently related event of Saudi history. The story tells how the twenty-two year old heir to the Saudi heritage set forth secretly by camel with thirty friends, his brother Muhammad and his cousin Abdullah bin Jiluwi. They left the family's place of exile in Kuwait, and crossed the desert, riding at night. Abdul Aziz left the bulk of his party in a palm grove south of Riyadh and continued on foot with a small raiding party. Part of this force concealed themselves close to the city walls, and he and nine men then made their way over the rooftops to the house of the Rashidi governor, Ajlan. Having discovered that the governor was asleep in Musmak fortress, he brought in his reserve party, and then regrouped his small force in a house on the central marketplace, opposite the gate of the fortress. At dawn the postern gate would be opened, and maybe they could surprise the guard. They burst into the fortress just as Ajlan was crossing the courtyard to breakfast. In the skirmish that followed Ajlan was killed by Abdullah bin Jiluwi. A spearpoint is still visible today, embedded during that foray in the gate of Musmak fortress. That very morning the people of Riyadh were proclaiming the return of the Saudis. The city's subsequent history has been closely associated with the resurgence of the House of Saud.

Today King Abdul Aziz al Saud (or "ibn Saud") is known as the unifier of the Arabian peninsula. First he defeated the Rashidi forces with his Ikhwan ("brethren") movement of tribal military cadres (or "Hijrahs"). Then the Hasa and Gulf region to the east, dominated by the Turks, fell under his control. Then the Hijaz and the Holy Cities accepted his rule.

But already in 1911, when the majestic concept of a Saudi state spanning Arabia was still far from a reality, Abdul Aziz had begun to reconstruct Riyadh as its capital. The old Qasr was rebuilt as the seat of government and Musmak fortress was used as a prison. The Qasr was extended so that it dominated the town by its size and height. The audience chamber, it was said, could accommodate three thousand people. The city walls were given towers at their corners.

By the time the very first cars reached Riyadh (in 1934), King Abdul Aziz had built an overhead walkway from his Murabba Palace to the mosque.

The vast gates of tamarisk wood were clad in iron – Bab Mazbah to the west, Shumaysi facing southwest, Bab Dakhna to the south, Al Suwaylim to the northeast, and the main gate, Thumairi, named after a hero of Abdul Aziz's raiding party, facing east.

H.St John Philby, the English traveller and companion of Abdul Aziz, published his impressions of daily life in Riyadh at this significant period of its history. At the heart of the city was the market place, occupying the entire open space to the north of the royal palace and divided into two sections, one of which was reserved exclusively for the use of women. The other, larger section comprised perhaps 120 shops, selling a miscellaneous assortment of goods "ranging from imported piece goods and indigenous leather-work and saddlery ... to such articles of luxury or desire as rifles, ammunition, watches and field glasses ... The thoroughfare is blocked by droves of sheep ... Here and there a shopman or paid hawker passes in and out among the clamouring crowd with a rifle or a pair of field glasses, or a mantle of Hasa workmanship crying the latest price bid and endeavouring to get a better offer." But at the hours of prayer this scene would be dramatically transformed: "In a moment the streets are filled with people decorously stalking with downcast eyes towards the mosques, and thereafter the silence is broken only by the deep responses of a dozen congregations."

He also described the Great Mosque, the main entrance of which faced the market place, as a rectangular building, measuring some sixty metres by fifty in area, and divided into three sections. Two of these were covered by low, flat roofs for prayers during the hot hours of

Murabba Palace (left, above *and* below), *now finely restored, was King Abdul Aziz's home from the 1930s to his death in 1953.*

"There is no building in all his territories so splendid in its proportion, so beautiful and representative of all that is best in modern Arabian architecture as the royal palace of Ibn Sa'ud."

the day. The central section was an open courtyard edged by colonnades of pointed arches typical of Wahhabi architecture. Instead of a minaret there was "a low stepped structure ... at the centre of the north side of the building."

The royal palace was incomparable: "There is no building in all his territories so splendid in its proportions, so beautiful and representative of all that is best in modern Arabian architecture ... Its merit lies in its extreme simplicity of design and in an almost complete absence of ornament." This was Murabba. Private apartments for King Abdul Aziz

("ibn Saud"), his family and staff were in the western wing and central section of the building, with adjoining audience chambers and offices in the north section. The eastern wing was reserved for domestic staff, with kitchens and stables to the south-east. Philby described the "spacious turret at the corner, the great expanse of clay wall, with its minute triangular perforations and surmounting fringe of stepped pinnacles" of the palace's impressive facade as seen from the main street. On hot evenings the inhabitants would lie out on the palace roofs to enjoy the cool of the evening.

These were illuminated by a great arc-lamp from Bombay which, every night, was set up on a tall pole; "ordinarily the lamp was lowered and extinguished somewhat before midnight or when ibn Sa'ud retired to his bed, but during the month of *Ramadan* the great light was left there all night to illuminate the praying congregation."

During the 1920s, Abdul Aziz had established radio links between the cities of his new demesne, bringing Riyadh in contact with outlying districts, and with the outside world. Only in 1932 was the Kingdom proclaimed – around the time

The United Nations Programme headquarters (above) *shares with the magnificent new Ministry of Foreign Affairs* (right – *and also on* pages 60-61) *a stylistic obeisance to the traditional architecture of central Arabia and Islam.*

the first automobile arrived in Riyadh, and still six years before the discovery of oil in Dhahran. Even then, the natural resource of this "black gold" had to wait until after the end of the Second World War to be effectively exploited.

As more Ministries were transferred from Jeddah to the capital, and as the oil industry developed, so Riyadh's population rose and the city grew to accommodate them. Significantly, in 1944, the

old city walls were demolished to make way for expansion and modernisation. A six hundred kilometre railway linking Riyadh to the Gulf Coast at Dammam was opened in 1951 – King Abdul Aziz's last public ceremony in the city – and the first airport was inaugurated in 1953, the year of the Founder-King's death. These made Riyadh more accessible and helped to speed its growth.

Electricity replaced kerosene lamps, asphalt roads were laid on sandy tracks and sewage systems and motorized water pumps were installed. Schools and colleges were established, hospitals and ministerial buildings rapidly followed. Newspapers made their appearance, and then television. In the decade to 1965 the population had doubled to an estimated

218,000.

But the years of greatest construction and development have undoubtedly been those following the 1968 city plan and the October, 1973, leap in oil prices. The transformation of the city was astonishing. From 1975 Riyadh became known as "the largest building site in the world". Seventy permits a day were being issued. The scale and pace were unprecedented, and, in these early years of frenetic development, it is said that Riyadh citizens returning after more than a year's absence were unable to find their way home through the changed streets.

However rapidly, modern villas were built, each with its own space for a garden. In the early days of rapid expan-

Najdi architectural styles are preserved in the "Grand Festival Palace" at Sulaimaniya (left *and* right) – *often rented for weddings and social events.*

sion lower-income housing areas to the east and south for immigrant workers suffered from inadequate planning. But from the start, land use was carefully defined to ensure that there were areas for schools, hospitals, mosques, gardens and playgrounds. Planners and architects alike created an elegant and efficient modern capital whose characteristics both in concept and detail recalled Riyadh's role in Islam, and its Najdi setting.

Today, although most of the palm-groves of a century ago no longer exist, Riyadh has been carefully cultivated as a garden city in the desert. One hundred and twenty children's playgrounds and twelve parks have been laid out and planted, and the site of the old airport began to be transformed in the early 1980s into the spacious Mannakh Al-Malik Abdul Aziz Gardens and a zoo. Flowerbeds, trees and fountains provide

Traditional Riyadh lives on today at many sites, such as the great Friday Mosque (top left) *and the clock tower at Al Adl square where justice is meted out. Above, the fine mosque in Murabba, where King Abdul Aziz worshipped, is still a centre of devotion to God. Nearby, the new complex at Al Hukm* (below) *combines the Governorate Building with the Palace of Justice, the municipal headquarters, the Police Department, and the King Abdul Aziz Cultural Centre.*

The Thumairi Gate (above) *is the first of five main gates of old Riyadh (and a sixth smaller one) to be rebuilt. The Nasiriyah Gate* (right), *specifically built as a ceremonial arch, stands in its own park. The Red Palace,* below, *close to Murabba, was once home to King Sa'ud bin Abdul Aziz.*

colour and freshness.

Traffic systems were constructed; a ninety-three kilometre, six-lane ring road now girdles the city, and links it to the inter-peninsula highways.

Architecture is the most public art, and the new capital, both in the detail of a shutter and in the grand plan of an entire complex, is unified by characteristic Islamic designs. In sheer scale

and formal beauty, many of Riyadh's new public buildings are unsurpassed elsewhere. The King Khalid airport, which opened in 1983, is itself a small city covering 225 square kilometres. The Conference Palace in Al Nasiriyah is the largest in the Middle East. The 170-metre television transmission tower at the Ministry of Information is the major landmark of the city. Its glass globe, sparkling like a diamond in the sunlight, is large enough to include a resturant and kitchens. The King Faisal Foundation comprises an Islamic research centre, a mosque, extensive office space, a conference hall and a shopping mall. The Diplomatic Quarter houses the embassies of some one hundred countries and a number of luxury international

(Opposite page) *The gateway of today's Riyadh is King Khalid International Airport, one of the architectural wonders of the world, of which the Royal Pavilion, seen here, is a smaller version of the main passenger terminals. It opened in 1984. Riyadh's first airport (partially re-planned as a zoo-park) opened in 1952.*

hotels cater for visitors.

No roads led to Riyadh at the beginning of the century. Now, its desert isolation has ended and it is one of the world's most important capital cities. If the King who made it the capital of Saudi Arabia could survey his nation from the Television Tower, he would be astonished by the glittering vision created out of the desert by his inheritors.

RIYADH
PORTRAYED

Among Riyadh's first class hotels are numbered – reading anti-clockwise from the top of the page – the Al Khozama, the Marriott, the Inter-Continental, the Minhal, the Atallah Sheraton, the Hyatt Regency, and the Riyadh Palace, fronted like an open book. Others include the Salahuddin in the north of the city.

During recent decades, Saudi trade has developed from the traditional *souk* to modern international commercial organisations exemplified – in real estate terms – in elegant steel and glass structures (as above), *the Abanumy Centre* (right) *on Siteen Street and the Al Rashid Trading and Contracting offices* (opposite) *on Dabab Street.*

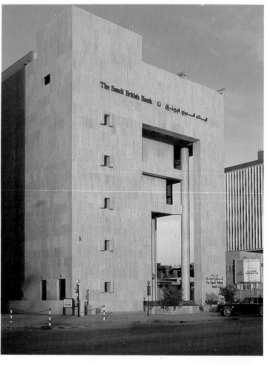

Opposite: *banks make their presence felt in large parts of central Riyadh – for example the National Commercial Bank with its green rooftop logo, the Saudi Investment Bank, Albank Alsaudi Alhollandi (the Dutch*

Bank), the Saudi British Bank and the Saudi American Bank. Sensitive planning has preserved the Najdi flavour in many of Riyadh's outstanding modern buildings, such as Petromin's headquarters, above.

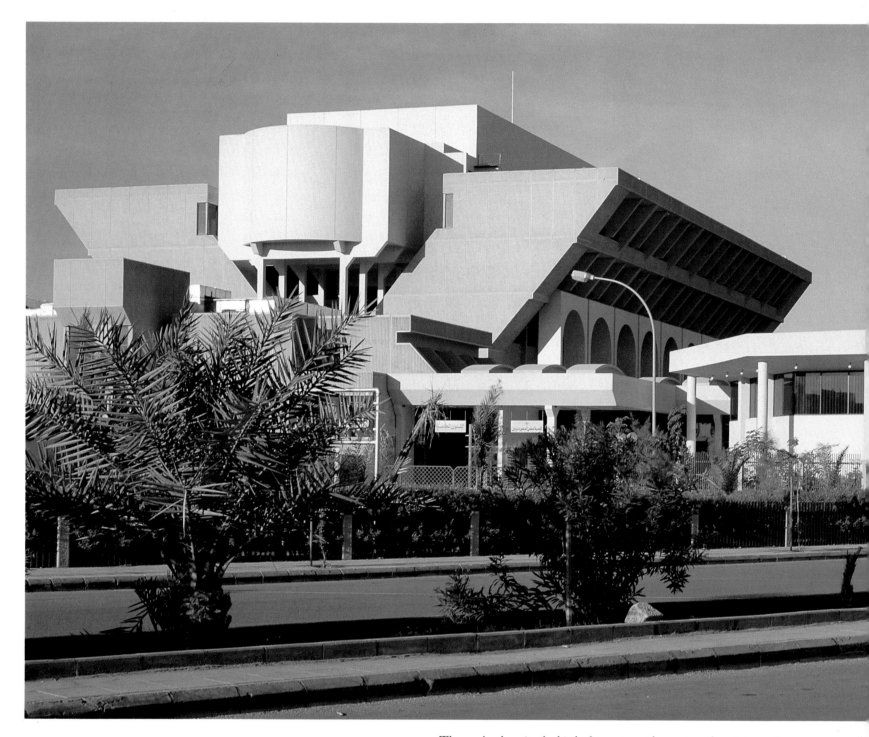

The sun's glare in the high clear atmosphere gives the city's modern architecture its strong clean lines and a constant call for shade, as in the Passport Office on Makkah Road, above, *and its adjacent mosque.*

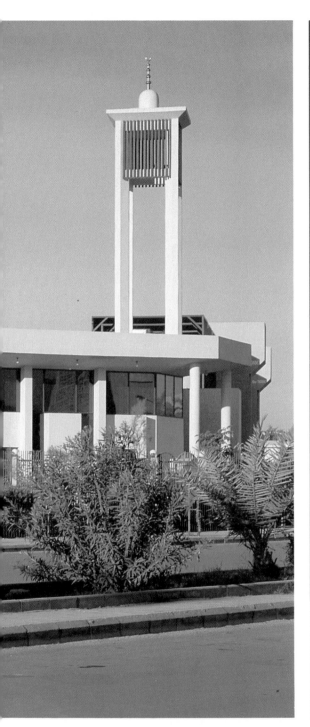

The national headquarters of the Port Authority, above and left, is composed of elegant mounted blocks, clad in subtly toned stone.

The Ministry of Foreign Affairs, just east of the Al Asima Gate, is clad in marble, and reflects many features of traditional Arab design – spare, fortress-like, clean-lined, beautifully proportioned. The only ornaments added to the design of the architect, Henning Larsen, are plaster panels carved by Moroccan craftsmen.

Setting the tone of confidence and elegance in public buildings are the Ministry of Post, Telegraph and Telephone (right), and below, *in anticlockwise sequence, the Royal Commission for Jubail and Yanbu,* SAMA's *headquarters in Al Mutamarat, the headquarters of the General Organisation of Social Insurance on Shara Matar, and* SABIC *headquarters in Al Murabba.*

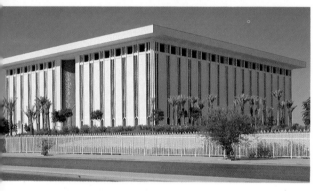

The magnificent Conference Palace, the adjacent Royal Conference Hall, and their mosque (above *and* left) *have become the jewel of the traditionally royal Nasiriyah area.*

Discipline and endeavour are symbolised outside the headquarters of the Presidency of Youth Welfare on Al Jamiah (or University) Street, below; *and the soaring spirit of competitive sport in the monument,* left, *at the Stadium.*
Opposite: *This elegant monument in the residential area of Sulaimaniya celebrates the Arabs' contribution of the arch to architecture.*

Dominated by the soaring 170-metre Television Tower, with its jewel-shaped observation capsule (opposite, left and top), the Ministry of Information's complex in Riyadh is the brain centre of television and radio broadcasting throughout the Kingdom.

Crowds of enthusiasts pack the stands of Riyadh's new International Stadium, off the Dammam Road, when the home team is playing. Saudi Arabia's international distinction at soccer was established beyond dispute at the 1984 Olympics. Riyadh is also the site of one of the country's three Sports Cities – the creation of the General Presidency for Youth Welfare. Athletics is probably the next most popular field of competitive sport, with volleyball, handball, gymnastics, basketball, swimming, table tennis and bicycling all playing a major part in the life of young Riyadhis.

Arabia has had immemorially long association with the horse – and is
mother of the Arab breed. On these pages this devotion is seen celebrated
on the race course in Malaz. There is no betting: the privilege of winning
suffices.

Riyadh contains several stables and riding clubs, like that east of Arba'een Street above and right – *or the Equestrian Club,* opposite below, *in Malaz. And if the funfairs (as* opposite) *and tennis clubs (as* below) *do not meet your needs, there is always the surrounding desert for some land-sailing (below right).*

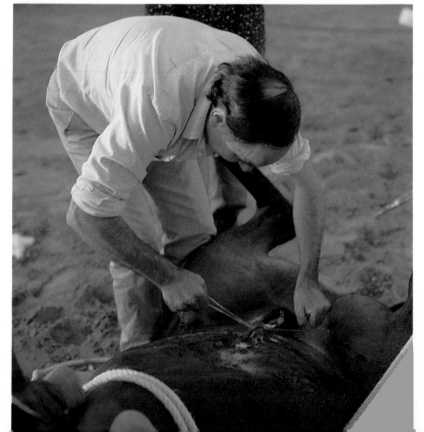

Many a Riyadhi is a horse-owner. Among the fine points of the legendary 'Arab' (opposite left) are a head held high, oblique shoulders, short back, long croup. The breed is known for its stamina. Veterinary surgeons (left) are in demand. Arabia's desert dog, the saluki, *is extremely fleet of foot. And beyond the city limits, the camel, humiliated by the motor vehicle above, is still king.*

After hunting – with falcon or saluki – camel racing has surely been the sport most closely associated with Arabia. At Janadriyah, on the edge of Riyadh, the annual camel races attract over 2,000 competitors. The twelve mile (19km) course is usually covered by the winner in about 42 minutes, with the skilled riders very often as young as eleven. It is an occasion for royalty, townsmen and Bedouin alike – and brass bands too.

On a Friday picnic beyond the city limits, a reservoir at Diriyah (above *and* opposite top) *provides as good a site as any for a splash and a swim. An empty car park serves for a game of improvised soccer practice* (left), *when one has grown out of the playground chute* (right).

On Friday – the day of worship and rest – some Riyadhi girls find time to play with younger sisters. Every district of the capital has its green parks, like that in Malaz, seen opposite. *Riyadh's municipality even has its own plant nursery.*

Nasiriyah's mosques bring to the worship of God an incomparable beauty and serenity, as glimpsed on these pages. There are 1245 mosques in Riyadh, and over 2,000 imams, muezzins, and other permanent staff, and many more employed on an irregular basis. Every mosque, great and small alike, has its minaret, and library, and washing area.

For those arriving or leaving Riyadh – or those who work at the site – the exquisite mosque at the King Khalid Airport provides the point of worship. It is a vast hexagon that can hold 5,000, its seemingly floating geodesic dome 33 metres across, triangulated by over a thousand panels of shining brass which (in the picture) have taken on the prevailing soft green of the lights.

The King Faisal Foundation in Oleya, the Islamic research centre (left and above), with its mosque, flats and shops, was inspired by hands cupped in prayer. A tented motif surmounts the stands and the entrance to the International Stadium (top and right).

55

Riyadh, the capital, preserves the great Saudi tradition of the ardah, *at the annual Cultural Festival at Al Janadriyah and elsewhere. The ballads of past glories are retold in song and mime to throbbing drums in imaginative costumes lovingly made for the occasion.*

*In rhythmic dance and antiphonal chant, and
with feint and assault, the dancing heritage of
Saudi Arabia's tribes lives on at Al Janadriyah,*
above *and* right, *and at Eid festivals.*

Staider entertainment is provided by fiddle and the nine-string sitara at a social function, above. *For a wedding among an immigrant Arab community (from Eritrea) nothing is spared to ensure that all look their prettiest.*

"Riyadh Yesterday and Today" has toured the world as an exhibition, showing the wonders of the city. HRH Prince Salman bin Abdul Aziz, Governor of Riyadh, was joined at its London opening by Prince Charles and Princess Diana (right). Below, a Riyadh suburb takes shape in maquette and, opposite, in real life. The Ministry of Foreign Affairs housing development in Oleya (opposite above) covers 39 hectares of land.

As the capital's population doubled, then re-doubled, all in two decades, an intense programme of building provided flats for new residents, such as the vast spiralled King's Building, (above and right), the tower block complex off Dabab Street (opposite, below), and many elegant terraced apartments like that of the Saudi Real Estate Company, (far right), and the Al Khozama Centre in Oleya. Riyadh today contains 17 sub-municipalities.

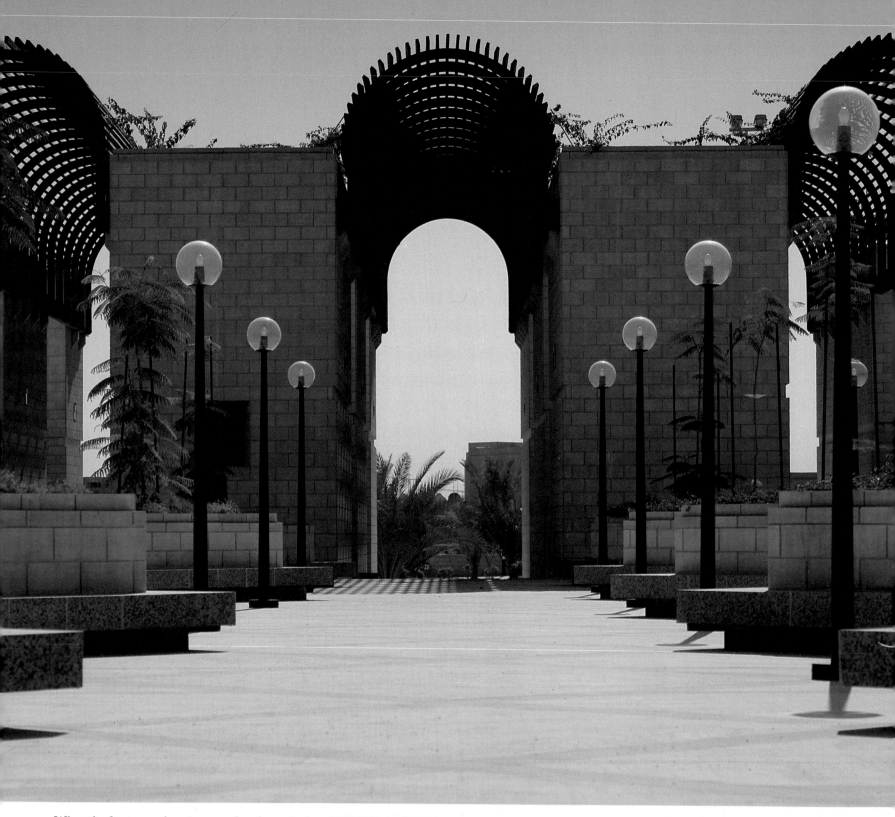

When the foreign embassies moved to the capital
from Jiddah in the mid-1980s, they were
provided with their own Diplomatic Quarter in
the north-east of the city, laid out with grace and
spaciousness, with elegant promenades (as
above). The Quarter is entered (right) from
the Hejaz Freeway.

Designed as the home for 30,000 – including families and staff – and 130 embassies, the Diplomatic Quarter has many communal facilities such as the magnificent sports centre, and the Diplomatic Club (seen above *and in the background,* left*).*

In the Diplomatic Quarter, each country's designated area – like that of the Americans (above and right) – is inventively planted with what best flourishes in the high, dry climate. Meanwhile an area of 900,000 square metres surrounding the Quarter is being landscaped with desert plants.

The design of each embassy was left to the country concerned, as, for instance, (top) the Japanese Embassy; and (above) the British – each, perhaps, reflecting the national outlook?

Tumbling water and a blaze of flowers greet those arriving – left – at the capital's King Khalid Airport. Those leaving (above) are likewise accorded space and elegance in an airport designed to handle 15 million passengers a year by the turn of the century.

"We paid careful attention to several Islamic forms – the arch, the dome, and of course, use of geometry." So said the leader of the architectural team, Gyo Obata, which designed King Khalid Airport. Seen opposite *is the control tower and,* below, *the Royal Pavilion, and a passenger concourse with a typical mosaic mural* (left).

For the mosque at the airport, travertine marble was quarried in Italy then shipped to England where it was etched with kufic script. Marble facing the outside walls was carved with floral designs in Italy. The immense hexagonal carpet bathing the floor in a glowing blue was woven in Hong Kong. Boston's Vesti Corporation designed and fabricated these components and others overleaf.

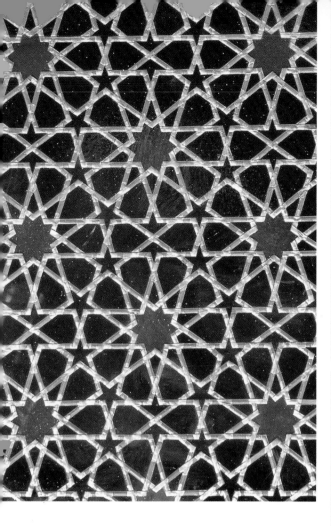

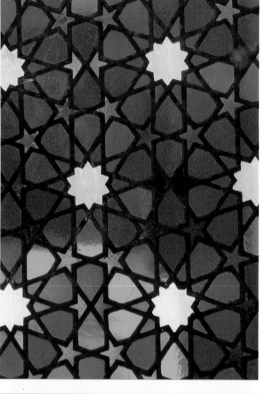
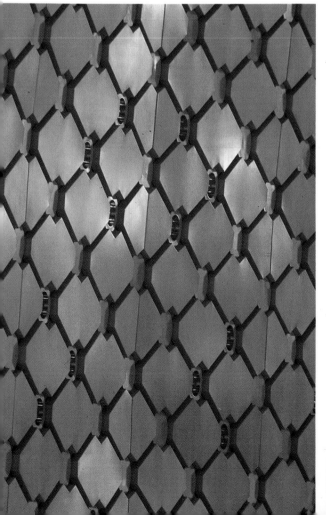

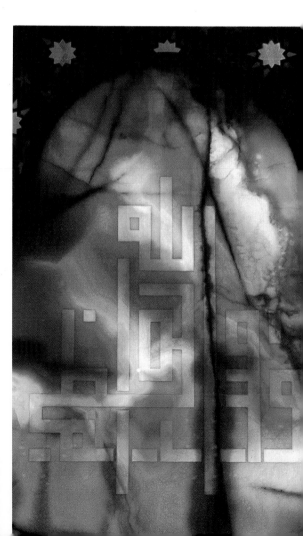

Woodworking companies in Syria, Jiddah, and Switzerland devoted their skills to the teak and mahogany doors seen on this page. Details of the Airport's exquisite beauty, which includes a brilliant variety of geometric glasswork, tiling and panelling, and an onyx window telling of man's devotion to God, are seen opposite and below.

Right: *The airport's panoply under a night sky. Construction presented massive problems of planning and economic analysis. Bechtel Civil Inc., designer and project manager, met the challenge by installing a powerful on-site computer, linked by satellite relay systems to control offices around the world. Shipments were then tracked from, variously, Spain and Greece, Japan and Korea, the United States and the United Kingdom. 'KKIA', as it is popularly known, opened to international traffic in 1984, and by 1987 there were 22 airlines flying regular routes to Riyadh, with Saudia accounting for 175 of the 195 daily international and domestic flights out of the airport, and having exclusive use of two of the four terminal buildings.*

Riyadh's King Saud University was founded in 1957 by royal decree of the late King Saud, portrayed above (on the right), *with his father King Abdul Aziz, and with Saudi Arabia's present King Fahd bin Abdul Aziz and Crown Prince Abdullah bin Abdul Aziz. It moved to its present 9 million square metre site on the Diriyah Road north of the city, in the early 1980s.* Below, *students cross the cloisters between the colleges.*

King Saud University's eastern entrance is dominated by a vast open book clothed in marble. Its great mosque below, *exemplifies the Islamic principles on which the country's higher education is based. The new campus' opening by King Fahd is commemorated* right.

King Saud University comprises 17 colleges each with its separate field of study, together with a centre for university studies for women and an Arabic language institute. These are situated along covered walkways (far left) *and shady cloisters* (above right), *which meet at the 'forum'* (centre, top).

The 'forum' is the main, formal entrance to the campus (top right), sited at the end of a long ceremonial road. The interior (above) is a lofty open space with a glass roof and inlaid marble floor. Grouped around it are communal buildings including the Student's Union, auditoriums, the dining hall, the university library, administration offices and the mosque.

Tapestries from France and sculpture, such as that seen right, *composed from Arabic numerals provide decoration.*

Senior school pupils (left) in Riyadh are now able to choose between the King Saud University, the Imam Muhammad Ibn Saud Islamic University (inaugurated in 1974) and vocational training colleges.

Education begins at a kindergarten, followed by primary, intermediate and secondary levels. Library study (above) *provides an opportunity for comparing notes. After one year at secondary level, pupils choose between science and literary subjects. Such cheerful and up-to-date school complexes as those* opposite *provide the best in modern education at all levels for over two thousand pupils.*

Several vocational colleges in Riyadh provide alternative higher education opportunities, including the Centre for Modern Design, left. The main public library (top) offers facilities to the general population.

Some of the world's most advanced hospitals are today found in Riyadh. The King Faisal Specialist Hospital and Medical Centre opened in 1975. Set in a garden (above) and with a welcoming entrance hall (left), it has 500 beds and advanced facilities which extend to open-heart surgery and cancer treatment in the Cancer Research Institute, opened in 1980. This is equipped with a 'cyclotron' for the most advanced diagnosis and treatment of cancers.

The King Khalid Eye Specialist Hospital (below *and* right, top *and* centre) *is the largest of its kind in the world. Opened in 1982, it is the base for a kingdom-wide eye-health care scheme in a region long plagued*

by eye disease. It has facilities to train Saudi ophthalmologists. Riyadh has five public hospitals, four private hospitals such as that in Oleya (right below) and 24 Health Care Centres.

In traditional Riyadhi commerce, the gold souk (above) *and the rugs market* (right) *are famous throughout the Arab world.*

To the resident of Riyadh, the elegance and the splendour of the home takes precedence – as suggested by the shop selling quality lighting, above *and* right. Far right: *in the Deira souk, a costume dealer still finds customers for the beautifully embroidered* bisht.

Tradition holds firm in downtown souks, where Bedouin camel bags, pack saddles, and saddle frames (above) are sought, and incense burners and brass goblets, too (right).

A young Riyadhi settles for a pastel-shade thobe, *and a cool white* ghotra *for the hot months, in preference to the (usually heavier) red and white chequered headcloth.* Right: *for the traditional deep bake-oven, a long-handled pan is essential.*

For traditional homes, incense from burners (left) *pervades the inner rooms, while cardomom-flavoured* gahwa *is served from beak-spouted coffee pots* (above), *whose built-in rattle within the lid reinforces through the ears the sense of homely comfort and refreshment to come.*

*Friday evening in Safar Square is the time and the place to buy your hunting falcon, of which the peregrine (*shahin*) and the* sakr *(or* hurr*) are usually favoured.*

The traditional life of which Riyadh was until recently the regional centre is kept alive at the "Cultural Village" of Janadriyah, on the north-eastern perimeter of the city. Here – by royal command – woodworkers, potters, swordsmiths, harness-makers, coppersmiths, and weavers are gathered under the aegis of the National Guard to remind Riyadhis how their fathers lived, and to ensure the survival of skills and techniques.

Riyadh has its archaeological and ethnological museum at Shemaisi (samples, top), and several other institutions ensuring the preservation of the past, such as the Museum of Popular Art (above), Musmak Fortress (above right), and the crafts centre at Janadriyah (right).

The old life is instantly recoverable by the visitor to Diriyah, where a well and traditional wellhead are pictured above. *The old well at Musmak Fortress, now restored, may be seen* left.

Riyadh is a city of manufacture. The Riyadh interests of SABIC (Saudi Basic Industries Corporation), for instance, embrace petrochemical and steel production. Other industries include water and plastics. Cement is produced at the Al Yamamah plant, above. *Alternative power sources from solar energy are being studied* (opposite, top) *by SOLERAS (Solar Energy Research American-Saudi). By-products of the petroleum industry include lubricants* (opposite, below).

Industrial areas on the perimeter of the city provide space and power facilities for new and expanding industries, such as the Al Kharj steel products company above. Pepsi-Cola chose Al Asha Road, in Az Zahra, for its bottling plant (right).

Riyadh's Petromin centre produces liquid petroleum gas, kerosene, aircraft fuel, diesel and asphalt, as well as gasoline for the city's cars, distributed through modern filling stations such as that on Al Ma'dhar Road (above). The antique Rolls Royce (right) at the car souk in Al Naseem recalls the arrival of the first automobile in Riyadh in 1934.

Riyadh has over 300 buses, including the ubiquitous yellow bluebird vehicles (top) and the Saudi Public Transport Company buses (centre). The Fire Department runs a fleet of yellow fire engines (bottom).

Dusk falls over today's Riyadh (above), *with its system of flyovers and the 93-kilometre ring road, and the elegant Television Tower rising above the skyline. Modern city life involves automatic bank machines and car-phones* (right).

The highway, left, to Taif, Makkah and Jiddah, sweeps down from Riyadh's escarpment. For an expanding city, construction work on new highways must continue (above): *foundations of gravel are laid* (opposite top) *after powerful pneumatic drills and diggers* (opposite below) *have cleared the way forward. Riyadh has a 93km ring road.*